Yeah, That Happened
My Terrifically Terrible Toddler

Created by
Erika Ehren

Copyright © 2011 by Erika Ehren

ALL RIGHTS RESERVED

ISBN   978-1-105-01971-5

Table of Contents

Worst Photo	5
Diaper Disasters	6
Potty Training Troubles	7
Biggest Mess Ever	8
Most Creative Outfit	9
Yuck! Funny Food Reactions	10
Bedtime Rituals Gone Awry	11
The Worst Night We Never Slept	12
Bathtime Tales	13
Most Expensive Thing Ever Broken	14
First Lies	15
Swearing Like a Sailor	16
Worst Tantrum	17

Here's Why Other People Can't Be Trusted to Watch My Kid	18
Playground Scuffles	19
Kids and Restaurants Don't Mix	20
Traveling With Kids Ain't Easy	21
Habits, Hobbies, and Obsessions	22
The Gifts That Went to Waste	23
Imaginary Friends	24
I Really Wanted to Throw Away	25
Songs, TV Shows, and Movies We Grown-Ups Grew To Hate	26
Sibling Rivalry	27
My Little Stand-Up Comedian	28
Made Up Words and Funny Pronunciations	29
It Scared Me to Death When	30
Embarrassing Honesty	31
Bad Little Parrot	32
Quotes	33-34

Worst Photo

Diaper Disasters

Potty Training Troubles

Biggest Mess Ever

Most Creative Outfit

Yuck! Funny Food Reactions

Bedtime Rituals Gone Awry

The Worst Night We Never Slept

Bathtime Tales

Most Expensive Thing Ever Broken

First Lies

Swearing Like a Sailor

Worst Tantrum

Here's Why Other People Can't Be Trusted to Watch My Kid

Playground Scuffles

Kids and Restaurants Don't Mix

Traveling With Kids Ain't Easy

Habits, Hobbies, and Obsessions

The Gifts That Went to Waste

Imaginary Friends

I Really Wanted to Throw Away

Songs, TV Shows, and Movies We Grown-Ups Grew to Hate

Sibling Rivalry

My Little Stand-Up Comedian

Made Up Words

Funny Pronunciations

It Scared Me to Death When

Embarrassing Honesty

Bad Little Parrot

Quotes

Quotes

www.ingramcontent.com/pod-product-compliance
Lightning Source LLC
Chambersburg PA
CBHW041702160426
43202CB00002B/14